Ella Goes to the Park

A Book about Shapes

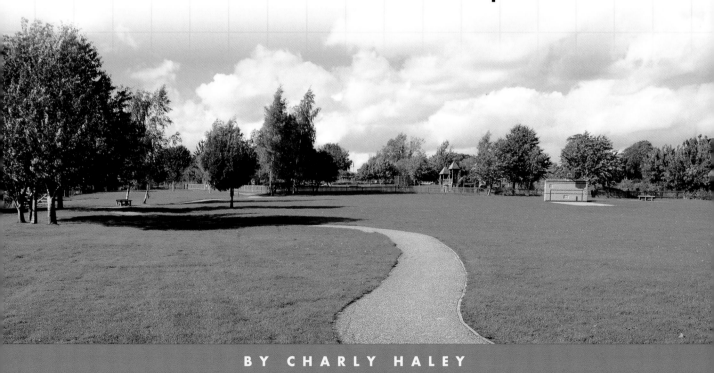

BY CHARLY HALEY

The Child's World®
childsworld.com

Published by The Child's World®
1980 Lookout Drive • Mankato, MN 56003-1705
800-599-READ • www.childsworld.com

Photographs ©: iStockphoto, cover (foreground), 3, 5,
6, 13; Braun S./iStockphoto, cover (background), 1;
Dmitry Pichugin/Shutterstock Images, 9 (background);
Nata Smilyk/Shutterstock Images, 9 (foreground), 10
(foreground), 14 (foreground), 16, 18 (foreground);
Shutterstock Images, 10 (background), 14 (background),
17; Halchynska Kseniia/Shutterstock Images, 18
(background); Paul Vasarhelyi/Shutterstock Images, 21

ISBN HARDCOVER: 9781503824874
ISBN PAPERBACK: 9781622434213
LCCN 2017964136

Printed in the United States of America
PA02387

About the Author

Charly Haley is a writer and children's book editor who lives in Minnesota. Aside from reading and writing, she enjoys music, yoga, and spending time with friends and family.

Today was
a big day
for Ella.
What did
Ella do today?

Ella went to the park with her dad.

Ella saw many different shapes at the park.

Ella saw a tree. The tree looked like a **triangle**.

Ella saw a brick wall. Each brick looked like a **rectangle**.

Ella's dad showed

her a tree stump.

The tree stump

looked like a **circle**.

Ella and her dad walked on a stone path. Each stone looked like a **square**.

Ella found a rock. The rock looked like an **oval**.

What shapes do you see
in the world around you?

Words to Know

circle (SIR-kuhl) A circle is a round shape. A coin has the shape of a circle.

oval (OH-vuhl) An oval is a long curved shape. Ella saw a rock that had the shape of an oval.

rectangle (REK-tang-guhl) A rectangle is a shape with four sides and four corners. Two of the sides in a rectangle are longer than the others.

square (SKWAYR) A square is a shape with four sides of the same length. A square is a special type of rectangle.

triangle (TRY-ang-ull) A triangle is a shape with three sides and three points. Anything with only three sides is a triangle.

Extended Learning Activities

1. Where do you see triangles and squares in your life?

2. Why do you think it is important to know the different shapes? How are shapes useful?

3. Have you ever tried to build things out of different shapes? What shapes work best for building?

To Learn More

Books

Barker, Stephen. *Chalkboard Shapes*. Lake Forest, CA: Walter Foster Jr., 2018.

Chernesky, Felicia Sanzari. *Pick a Circle, Gather Squares: A Fall Harvest of Shapes*. Chicago, IL: Albert Whitman & Company, 2013.

Walter, Jackie. *What Shape Is It?* London, UK: Hachette Children's, 2016.

Web Sites

Visit our Web site for links about shapes:

childsworld.com/links

Note to Parents, Teachers, and Librarians: We routinely verify our Web links to make sure they are safe and active sites. So encourage your readers to check them out!